DRIVING
MISS
DAISY

DRIVING
MISS
DAISY

ALFRED UHRY

THEATRE COMMUNICATIONS GROUP

Driving Miss Daisy is published by Theatre Communications Group, Inc.,
355 Lexington Ave., New York, NY 10017.

The publications and programs of Theatre Communications Group are supported by Actors' Equity Foundation, Alcoa Foundation, ARCO Foundation, AT&T Foundation, Center for Arts Criticism, Citicorp/Citibank, Columbia Pictures Entertainment, Consolidated Edison Company of New York, Eleanor Naylor Dana Charitable Trust, Dayton Hudson Foundation, Exxon Corporation, Home Box Office, Japan-U.S. Friendship Commission, Jerome Foundation, Joe and Emily Lowe Foundation, Andrew W. Mellon Foundation, Mobil Foundation, National Broadcasting Company, National Endowment for the Arts, New York City Department of Cultural Affairs, New York Community Trust, New York Life Foundation, New York State Council on the Arts, Pew Charitable Trusts, Philip Morris Companies, Rockefeller Foundation, Scherman Foundation, Shell Oil Company Foundation, Shubert Foundation, L. J. Skaggs and Mary C. Skaggs Foundation, Consulate General of Spain and Xerox Foundation.

Driving Miss Daisy was first produced Off Broadway by Playwrights Horizons, New York City in 1987. It was subsequently produced by Jane Harmon/Nina Keneally, Ivy Properties, Ltd./Richard Frankel, Gene Wolsk/Alan M. Shore and Susan S. Meyerberg, in association with Playwrights Horizons, Off Broadway in 1987.

On the Cover: Morgan Freeman and Dana Ivey;
photograph copyright © 1988 by Jack Mitchell.

Library of Congress Cataloging-in-Publication Data

Uhry, Alfred.

Driving Miss Daisy.

I. Title.

PS3571.H7D7   1988   812'.54—dc19   88-24836

ISBN 0-930452-88-7

ISBN 0-930452-89-5 (pbk.)

Design by The Sarabande Press

First Edition, September 1988

FOR MAMA AND WILL
R.I.P.

PREFACE

There was a real Miss Daisy. She was a friend of my
grandmother's in Atlanta, back in the forties when I was a
child. She was a "maiden lady" as we called it then, the
last of a big family, and she lived in what I remember as
a spooky old Victorian house. There was a Hoke, too. He
was the sometime bartender at our German-Jewish
country club, and, I believe, he supplemented his income
by bartending at private parties around town. And Boolie
. . . well, I didn't really know him, but he was the
brother of my dear Aunt Marjorie's friend Rosalie. They
were real people, all right, but I have used only their
names in creating the three characters in *Driving Miss
Daisy*. I wanted to use names that seemed particular to
the Atlanta I grew up in. The actual characters, though,
are made of little bits and pieces of my childhood. Quite

a bit of my grandmother, Lena Guthman Fox, and her four older sisters have gone into Miss Daisy herself. And I guess my mother, Alene Fox Uhry, is in there too. Hoke is based on my grandmother's chauffeur, Will Coleman, but also on Bill and Riley and Marvin and Pete and other black chauffeurs I knew in those days. And Boolie is so many pieces of so many men I know (including me, I suppose) that it would be hard for me to say what exactly comes from what.

I find that there is unusual interest in my offstage character Florine, Boolie's wife. Many people have said (by mail or in person) that they know Florine, she is their aunt, their cousin, their old friend from home, etc., etc., etc., and who was she really? I will never tell.

When I wrote this play I never dreamed I would be writing an introduction to it because I never thought it would get this far. The original schedule was a five-week run at Playwrights Horizons, a New York nonprofit theatre, in the spring of 1987, and I made sure various family members from Atlanta would get to town during that period. The theatre seated seventy-four people. Just the right size, I thought, for a little play that could surely have appeal only to me, my family, and a few other southerners. To my amazement, the appeal was much wider. When the five weeks was up, the engagement was extended for another five weeks, and by then the demand for tickets was so great that we had to move to a bigger theatre.

Flash forward a year and a half. Now there are several companies playing and many more productions planned in all parts of the world. I am in the process of writing the screenplay. I have won the Pulitzer Prize. Even as I write these words they seem unbelievable to me. When I wonder how all this happened (which I do a lot!) I can come up with only one answer. I wrote what I knew to be the truth and people have recognized it as such.

And I have been remarkably lucky. My wife, Joanna, has believed in me for thirty years. How can you ever thank somebody for that? And my daughters, Emily, Elizabeth, Kate and Nell, have always been loving and understanding about what I do for a living. Flora Roberts, my agent for twenty-five years, has always been my friend too, as well as a wonderful sounding board. I must also thank Jane Harmon, Robert Waldman, Andre Bishop, Ron Lagomarsino, Dana Ivey, Morgan Freeman, and Ray Gill for caring so much.

This has been one helluva ride!

—Alfred Uhry

CHARACTERS

DAISY WERTHAN   A WIDOW (AGE 72-97)
HOKE COLEBURN   HER CHAUFFEUR (AGE 60-85)
BOOLIE WERTHAN   HER SON (AGE 40-65)

TIME AND PLACE

THIS PLAY TAKES PLACE FROM 1948 TO 1973, MOSTLY IN
ATLANTA, GEORGIA. THERE ARE MANY LOCALES. THE
SCENERY IS MEANT TO BE SIMPLE AND EVOCATIVE. THE
ACTION SHIFTS FREQUENTLY AND, I HOPE, FLUIDLY.

In the dark we hear Daisy call from offstage: "Idella, I'm gone to market." A car ignition is turned on; then we hear a horrible crash, followed by bangs and booms and wood splintering. The very loud noise stops suddenly and the lights come up on Daisy Werthan's living room. Daisy, age seventy-two, is wearing a summer dress and high-heeled shoes. Her hair, her clothes, her walk, everything about her suggests bristle and feistiness and high energy. She appears to be in excellent health. Her son, Boolie Werthan, forty, is a businessman, Junior Chamber of Commerce style. He has a strong, capable air. The Werthans are Jewish, but they have strong Atlanta accents.

DAISY: No!
BOOLIE: Mama!
DAISY: No!

BOOLIE: Mama!

DAISY: I said no, Boolie, and that's the end of it.

BOOLIE: It's a miracle you're not laying in Emory Hospital—or decked out at the funeral home. Look at you! You didn't even break your glasses.

DAISY: It was the car's fault.

BOOLIE: Mama, the car didn't just back over the driveway and land on the Pollard's garage all by itself. You had it in the wrong gear.

DAISY: I did not!

BOOLIE: You put it in reverse instead of drive. The police report shows that.

DAISY: You should have let me keep my La Salle.

BOOLIE: Your La Salle was eight years old.

DAISY: I don't care. It never would have behaved this way. And you know it.

BOOLIE: Mama, cars don't behave. They are behaved upon. The fact is you, all by yourself, demolished that Packard.

DAISY: Think what you want. I know the truth.

BOOLIE: The truth is you shouldn't be allowed to drive a car anymore.

DAISY: No.

BOOLIE: Mama, we are just going to have to hire somebody to drive you.

DAISY: No *we* are not. This is my business.

BOOLIE: Your insurance policy is written so that they are going to have to give you a brand-new car.

DAISY: Not another Packard, I hope.

BOOLIE: Lord Almighty! Don't you see what I'm saying?

DAISY: Quit talking so ugly to your mother.

BOOLIE: Mama, you are seventy-two years old and you just cost the insurance company twenty-seven hundred dollars. You are a terrible risk. Nobody is going to issue you a policy after this.

DAISY: You're just saying that to be hateful.

BOOLIE: Okay. Yes. Yes I am. I'm making it all up. Every insurance company in America is lined up in the driveway waving their fountain pens and falling all over themselves to get you to sign on. Everybody wants Daisy Werthan, the only woman in the history of driving to demolish a three-week-old Packard, a two-car garage and a freestanding tool shed in one fell swoop!

DAISY: You talk so foolish sometimes, Boolie.

BOOLIE: And even if you could get a policy somewhere, it wouldn't be safe. I'd worry all the time. Look at how many of your friends have men to drive them. Miss Ida Jacobs, Miss Ethel Hess, Aunt Nonie —

DAISY: They're all rich.

BOOLIE: Daddy left you plenty enough for this. I'll do the interviewing at the plant. Oscar in the freight elevator knows every colored man in Atlanta worth talking about. I'm sure in two weeks' time I can find you somebody perfectly —

DAISY: No!

BOOLIE: You won't even have to do anything, Mama. I told you. I'll do all the interviewing, all the reference checking, all the —

DAISY: No. Now stop running your mouth! I am seventy-two years old as you so gallantly reminded me and I am a widow, but unless they rewrote the Constitution and didn't tell me, I still have rights. And one of my rights is the right to invite who I want—not who you want—into my house. You do accept the fact that this is my house? What I do not want—and absolutely will not have is some—*(She gropes for a bad-enough word)* some chauffeur sitting in my kitchen, gobbling my food, running up my phone bill. Oh, I hate all that in my house!

BOOLIE: You have Idella.

DAISY: Idella is different. She's been coming to me three times a week since you were in the eighth grade and we know how to stay out of each other's way. And even so there are nicks and chips in most of my wedding china and I've seen her throw silver forks in the garbage more than once.

BOOLIE: Do you think Idella has a vendetta against your silverware?

DAISY: Stop being sassy. You know what I mean. I was brought up to do for myself. On Forsyth Street we couldn't afford them and we did for ourselves. That's still the best way, if you ask me.

BOOLIE: Them! You sound like Governor Talmadge.

DAISY: Why, Boolie! What a thing to say! I'm not prejudiced! Aren't you ashamed?

BOOLIE: I've got to go home. Florine'll be having a fit.

DAISY: Y'all must have plans tonight.

BOOLIE: Going to the Ansleys for a dinner party.

DAISY: I see.

BOOLIE: You see what?

DAISY: The Ansleys. I'm sure Florine bought another new dress. This is her idea of heaven on earth, isn't it?

BOOLIE: What?

DAISY: Socializing with Episcopalians.

BOOLIE: You're a doodle, Mama. I guess Aunt Nonie can run you anywhere you need to go for the time being.

DAISY: I'll be fine.

BOOLIE: I'll stop by tomorrow evening.

DAISY: How do you know I'll be here? I'm certainly not dependent on you for company.

BOOLIE: Fine. I'll call first. And I still intend to interview colored men.

DAISY: No!

BOOLIE: Mama!

DAISY *(Singing to end discussion)*:
  After the ball is over
  After the break of morn
  After the dancers leaving
  After the stars are gone
  Many a heart is aching
  If you could read them all —

Lights fade on Daisy as she sings and come up on Boolie at the Werthan Company. He sits at a desk piled with papers, and speaks into an intercom.

BOOLIE: Okay, Miss McClatchey. Send him on in.

Boolie continues working at his desk. Hoke Coleburn enters, a black man of about sixty, dressed in a somewhat shiny suit and carrying a fedora, a man clearly down on his luck but anxious to keep up appearances.

  Yes, Hoke isn't it?

HOKE: Yassuh. Hoke Coleburn.

BOOLIE: Have a seat there. I've got to sign these letters. I don't want Miss McClatchey fussing at me.

HOKE: Keep right on with it. I got all the time in the worl'.

BOOLIE: I see. How long you been out of work?

HOKE: Since back befo' las' November.

BOOLIE: Long time.

HOKE: Well, Mist' Werthan, you try bein' me and looking for work. They hirin' young if they hirin' colored, an' they ain' even hirin' much young, seems like. (*Boolie is involved with his paperwork*) Mist' Werthan? Y'all people Jewish, ain' you?

BOOLIE: Yes we are. Why do you ask?

HOKE: I'd druther drive for Jews. People always talkin' 'bout they stingy and they cheap, but doan' say none of that roun' me.

BOOLIE: Good to know you feel that way. Now, tell me where you worked before.

HOKE: Yassuh. That what I'm gettin' at. One time I workin' for this woman over near Little Five Points. What was that woman's name? I forget. Anyway, she president of the Ladies Auxiliary over yonder to the Ponce De Leon Baptist Church and seem like she always bringing up God and Jesus and do unto others. You know what I'm talkin' 'bout?

BOOLIE: I'm not sure. Go on.

HOKE: Well, one day, Mist' Werthan, one day that woman say to me, she say "Hoke, come on back in the back wid me. I got something for you." And we go on back yonder and, Lawd have mercy, she have all these old shirts and collars be on the bed, yellow,

you know, and nasty like they been stuck off in a
chifferobe and forgot about. Thass right. And she say
"Ain' they nice? They b'long to my daddy befo' he
pass and we fixin' to sell 'em to you for twenty-five
cent apiece."

BOOLIE: What was her name?

HOKE: Thass what I'm thinkin'. What *was* that woman's
name? Anyway, as I was goin' on to say, any fool see
the whole bunch of them collars and shirts together
ain' worth a nickel! Them's the people das callin'
Jews cheap! So I say "Yassum, I think about it" and I
get me another job fas' as I can.

BOOLIE: Where was that?

HOKE: Mist' Harold Stone, Jewish gentleman jes' like
you. Judge, live over yonder on Lullwater Road.

BOOLIE: I knew Judge Stone.

HOKE: You doan' say! He done give me this suit when he
finish wid it. An' this necktie too.

BOOLIE: You drove for Judge Stone?

HOKE: Seven years to the day nearabout. An' I be there
still if he din' die, and Miz Stone decide to close up
the house and move to her people in Savannah. And
she say "Come on down to Savannah wid me, Hoke."
'Cause my wife dead by then and I say "No thank
you." I didn't want to leave my grandbabies and I
doan' get along with that Geechee trash they got
down there.

BOOLIE: Judge Stone was a friend of my father's.

HOKE: You doan' mean! Oscar say you need a driver for
yo' family. What I be doin'? Runnin' yo' children to
school and yo' wife to the beauty parlor and like dat?

BOOLIE: I don't have any children. But tell me—

HOKE: Thass a shame! My daughter bes' thing ever happen to me. But you young yet. I wouldn't worry none.

BOOLIE: I won't. Thank you. Did you have a job after Judge Stone?

HOKE: I drove a milk truck for the Avondale Dairy through the whole war—the one jes' was.

BOOLIE: Hoke, what I'm looking for is somebody to drive my mother around.

HOKE: Excuse me for askin', but how come she ain' hire fo' herseff?

BOOLIE: Well, it's a delicate situation.

HOKE: Mmmm-hmm. She done gone roun' the bend a little? That'll happen when they get on.

BOOLIE: Oh no. Nothing like that. She's all there. Too much there is the problem. It just isn't safe for her to drive anymore. She knows it, but she won't admit it. I'll be frank with you. I'm a little desperate.

HOKE: I know what you mean 'bout dat. Once I was outta work my wife said to me "Oooooh, Hoke, you ain' gon get now nother job." And I say "What you talkin' 'bout, woman?" And the very next week I go to work for that woman in Little Five Points. Cahill! Miz Frances Cahill. And then I go to Judge Stone and they the reason I happy to hear you Jews.

BOOLIE: Hoke, I want you to understand, my mother is a little high-strung. She doesn't want anybody driving her. But the fact is you'd be working for me. She can say anything she likes but she can't fire you. You understand?

HOKE: Sho I do. Don't worry none about it. I hold on no matter what way she run me. When I nothin' but a little boy down there on the farm above Macon, I use to wrastle hogs to the ground at killin' time, and ain' no hog get away from me yet.

BOOLIE: How does twenty dollars a week sound?

HOKE: Soun' like you got yo' mama a chauffeur.

Lights fade on them and come up on Daisy, who enters her living room with the morning paper. She reads with interest. Hoke enters the living room. He carries a chauffeur's cap instead of his hat. Daisy's concentration on the paper becomes fierce when she senses Hoke's presence.

Mornin', Miz Daisy.

DAISY: Good morning.

HOKE: Right cool in the night, wadn't it?

DAISY: I wouldn't know. I was asleep.

HOKE: Yassum. What yo' plans today?

DAISY: That's my business.

HOKE: You right about dat. Idella say we runnin' outta coffee and Dutch Cleanser.

DAISY: We?

HOKE: She say we low on silver polish too.

DAISY: Thank you. I will go to the Piggly Wiggly on the trolley this afternoon.

HOKE: Now, Miz Daisy, how come you doan' let me carry you?

DAISY: No, thank you.

HOKE: Ain't that what Mist' Werthan hire me for?

DAISY: That's his problem.

HOKE: All right den. I find something to do. I tend yo'
zinnias.

DAISY: Leave my flower bed alone.

HOKE: Yassum. You got a nice place back beyond the
garage ain' doin' nothin' but sittin' there. I could put
you in some butter beans and some tomatoes and
even some Irish potatoes could we get some ones
with good eyes.

DAISY: If I want a vegetable garden, I'll plant it for
myself.

HOKE: Well, I go out and set in the kitchen then, like I
been doin' all week.

DAISY: Don't talk to Idella. She has work to do.

HOKE: Nome. I jes' sit there till five o'clock.

DAISY: That's your affair.

HOKE: Seem a shame, do. That fine Oldsmobile settin'
out there in the garage. Ain't move a inch from
when Mist' Werthan rode it over here from Mitchell
Motors. Only got nineteen miles on it. Seem like
that insurance company give you a whole new car for
nothin'.

DAISY: That's your opinion.

HOKE: Yassum. And my other opinion is a fine rich
Jewish lady like you doan' b'long draggin' up the
steps of no bus, luggin' no grocery-store bags. I
come along and carry them fo' you.

DAISY: I don't need you. I don't want you. And I don't
like you saying I'm rich.

HOKE: I won' say it then.

DAISY: Is that what you and Idella talk about in the
kitchen? Oh, I hate this! I hate being discussed

behind my back in my own house! I was born on
Forsyth Street and, believe you me, I knew the value
of a penny. My brother Manny brought home a white
cat one day and Papa said we couldn't keep it because
we couldn't afford to feed it. My sisters saved up
money so I could go to school and be a teacher. We
didn't have anything!

HOKE: Yassum, but look like you doin' all right now.

DAISY: And I've ridden the trolley with groceries plenty
of times!

HOKE: Yassum, but I feel bad takin' Mist' Werthan's
money for doin' nothin'. You understand?

DAISY: How much does he pay you?

HOKE: That between me and him, Miz Daisy.

DAISY: Anything over seven dollars a week is robbery.
Highway robbery!

HOKE: Specially when I doan' do nothin' but set on a
stool in the kitchen all day long. Tell you what,
while you goin' on the trolley to the Piggly Wiggly,
I hose down yo' front steps.

Daisy is putting on her hat.

DAISY: All right.

HOKE: All right I hose yo' steps?

DAISY: All right the Piggly Wiggly. And then home.
Nowhere else.

HOKE: Yassum.

DAISY: Wait. You don't know how to run the
Oldsmobile!

HOKE: Miz Daisy, a gearshift like a third arm to me.
Anyway, thissun automatic. Any fool can run it.

DAISY: Any fool but me, apparently.

HOKE: Ain't no need to be so hard on yo'seff now. You cain' drive but you probably do alotta things I cain' do.

DAISY: The idea!

HOKE: It all work out.

DAISY *(Calling offstage)*: I'm gone to the market, Idella.

HOKE *(Also calling)*: And I right behind her!

Hoke puts on his cap and helps Daisy into the car. He sits at the wheel and backs the car down the driveway. Daisy, in the rear, is in full bristle.

I love a new car smell. Doan' you?

Daisy slides over to the other side of the seat.

DAISY: I'm nobody's fool, Hoke.

HOKE: Nome.

DAISY: I can see the speedometer as well as you can.

HOKE: I see dat.

DAISY: My husband taught me how to run a car.

HOKE: Yassum.

DAISY: I still remember everything he said. So don't you even think for a second that you can—wait! You're speeding! I see it!

HOKE: We ain't goin' but nineteen miles an hour.

DAISY: I like to go under the speed limit.

HOKE: Speed limit thirty-five here.

DAISY: The slower you go, the more you save on gas. My husband told me that.

HOKE: We barely movin'. Might as well walk to the Piggly Wiggly.

DAISY: Is this your car?

HOKE: Nome.

DAISY: Do you pay for the gas?

HOKE: Nome.

DAISY: All right then. My fine son may think I'm losing my abilities, but I am still in control of what goes on in my car. Where are you going?

HOKE: To the grocery store.

DAISY: Then why didn't you turn on Highland Avenue?

HOKE: Piggly Wiggly ain' on Highland Avenue. It on Euclid, down there near—

DAISY: I know where it is and I want to go to it the way I always go. On Highland Avenue.

HOKE: That three blocks out of the way, Miz Daisy.

DAISY: Go back! Go back this minute!

HOKE: We in the wrong lane! I cain' jes'—

DAISY: Go back I said! If you don't, I'll get out of this car and walk!

HOKE: We movin'! You cain' open the do'!

DAISY: This is wrong! Where are you taking me?

HOKE: The sto'.

DAISY: This is wrong. You have to go back to Highland Avenue!

HOKE: Mmmm-hmmmm.

DAISY: I've been driving to the Piggly Wiggly since the day they put it up and opened it for business. This isn't the way! Go back! Go back this minute!

HOKE: Yonder the Piggly Wiggly.

DAISY: Get ready to turn now.

HOKE: Yassum.

DAISY: Look out! There's a little boy behind that shopping cart!

HOKE: I see dat.

DAISY: Pull in next to the blue car.

HOKE: We closer to the do' right here.

DAISY: Next to the blue car! I don't park in the sun! It fades the upholstery.

HOKE: Yassum.

He pulls in, and gets out as Daisy springs out of the back seat.

DAISY: Wait a minute. Give me the car keys.

HOKE: Yassum.

DAISY: Stay right here by the car. And you don't have to tell everybody my business.

HOKE: Nome. Doan' forget the Dutch Cleanser now.

Daisy fixes him with a look meant to kill and exits. Hoke waits by the car for a minute, then hurries to the phone booth at the corner.

Hello? Miz McClatchey? Hoke Coleburn here. Can I speak to him? *(Pause)* Mornin' sir, Mist' Werthan. Guess where I'm at? I'm at dishere phone booth on Euclid Avenue right next to the Piggly Wiggly. I jes' drove yo' mama to the market. *(Pause)* She flap around some on the way. But she all right. She in the store. Uh-oh. Miz Daisy look out the store window and doan' see me, she liable to throw a fit right there by the checkout. *(Pause)* Yassuh, only took six days. Same time it take the Lawd to make the worl'.

Lights out on Hoke. We hear a choir singing.

ALFRED UHRY

CHOIR: May the words of my mouth
And the meditations of my heart
Be acceptable in Thy sight, O Lord
My strength and my redeemer. Amen.

Light up on Hoke waiting by the car, looking at a newspaper. Daisy enters in a different hat and a fur piece.

HOKE: How yo' temple this mornin', Miz Daisy?
DAISY: Why are you here?
HOKE *(Helping her into the car)*: I bring you to de temple like you tell me.
DAISY: I can get myself in. Just go. *(She makes a tight little social smile and a wave out the window)* Hurry up out of here!

Hoke starts up the car.

HOKE: Yassum.
DAISY: I didn't say speed. I said get me away from here.
HOKE: Somethin' wrong back yonder?
DAISY: No.
HOKE: Somethin' I done?
DAISY: No. *(A beat)* Yes.
HOKE: I ain' done nothin'!
DAISY: You had the car right in front of the front door of the temple! Like I was Queen of Romania! Everybody saw you! Didn't I tell you to wait for me in the back?
HOKE: I jes' tryin' to be nice. They two other chauffeurs right behind me.
DAISY: You made me look like a fool. A g.d. fool!

15

HOKE: Lawd knows you ain' no fool, Miz Daisy.

DAISY: Slow down. Miriam and Beulah and them, I could see what they were thinking when we came out of services.

HOKE: What that?

DAISY: That I'm trying to pretend I'm rich.

HOKE: You is rich, Miz Daisy!

DAISY: No I'm not! And nobody can ever say I put on airs. On Forsyth Street we only had meat once a week. We made a meal off of grits and gravy. I taught the fifth grade at the Crew Street School! I did without plenty of times, I can tell you.

HOKE: And now you doin' with. What so terrible in that?

DAISY: You! Why do I talk to you? You don't understand me.

HOKE: Nome, I don't. I truly don't. 'Cause if I ever was to get ahold of what you got I be shakin' it around for everybody in the world to see.

DAISY: That's vulgar. Don't talk to me!

Hoke mutters something under his breath.

What? What did you say? I heard that!

HOKE: Miz Daisy, you needs a chauffeur and Lawd know, I needs a job. Let's jes' leave it at dat.

Light out on them and up on Boolie, in his shirtsleeves. He has a phone to his ear.

BOOLIE: Good morning, Mama. What's the matter? *(Pause)* What? Mama, you're talking so fast I . . . .

What? All right. All right. I'll come by on my way to work. I'll be there as soon as I can.

Light out on him and up on Daisy, pacing around her house in a winter bathrobe. Boolie enters in a topcoat and scarf.

I didn't expect to find you in one piece.

DAISY: I wanted you to be here when he comes. I wanted you to hear it for yourself.

BOOLIE: Hear what? What is going on?

DAISY: He's stealing from me!

BOOLIE: Hoke? Are you sure?

DAISY: I don't make empty accusations. I have proof!

BOOLIE: What proof?

DAISY: This! *(She triumphantly pulls an empty can of salmon out of her robe pocket)* I caught him red-handed! I found this hidden in the garbage pail under some coffee grounds.

BOOLIE: You mean he stole a can of salmon?

DAISY: Here it is! Oh I knew. I knew something was funny. They all take things, you know. So I counted.

BOOLIE: You counted?

DAISY: The silverware first and the linen dinner napkins and then I went into the pantry. I turned on the light and the first thing that caught my eye was a hole behind the corned beef. And I knew right away. There were only eight cans of salmon. I had nine. Three for a dollar on sale.

BOOLIE: Very clever, Mama. You made me miss my breakfast and be late for a meeting at the bank for a thirty-three-cent can of salmon. *(He jams his hand in*

his pocket and pulls out some bills) Here! You want
thirty-three cents? Here's a dollar! Here's ten dollars!
Buy a pantry full of salmon!

DAISY: Why, Boolie! The idea! Waving money at me like
I don't know what! I don't want the money. I want
my things!

BOOLIE: One can of salmon?

DAISY: It was mine. I bought it and I put it there and he
went into my pantry and took it and he never said a
word. I leave him plenty of food every day and I
always tell him exactly what it is. They are like
having little children in the house. They want
something so they just take it. Not a smidgin of
manners. No conscience. He'll never admit this.
"Nome," he'll say. "I doan' know nothin' 'bout that."
And I don't like it! I don't like living this way! I
have no privacy.

BOOLIE: Mama!

DAISY: Go ahead. Defend him. You always do.

BOOLIE: All right. I give up. You want to drive yourself
again, you just go ahead and arrange it with the
insurance company. Take your blessed trolley. Buy
yourself a taxicab. Anything you want. Just leave me
out of it.

DAISY: Boolie . . .

Hoke enters in an overcoat.

HOKE: Mornin', Miz Daisy. I b'lieve it fixin' to clear up.
S'cuse me, I didn't know you was here Mist'
Werthan.

BOOLIE: Hoke, I think we have to have a talk.

HOKE: Jes' a minute. Lemme put my coat away. I be right back. *(He pulls a brown paper bag out of his overcoat)* Oh, Miz Daisy. Yestiddy when you out with yo' sister I ate a can o' your salmon. I know you say eat the leff-over pork chops, but they stiff. Here, I done buy you another can. You want me to put it in the pantry fo' you?

DAISY: Yes. Thank you, Hoke.

HOKE: I'll be right wit' you Mist' Werthan.

Hoke exits. Daisy looks at the empty can in her hand.

DAISY *(Trying for dignity)*: I've got to get dressed now. Goodbye, son.

She pecks his cheek and exits. Lights out on Boolie. We hear sounds of birds twittering. Lights come up brightly, indicating hot sun. Daisy, in a light dress, is kneeling, a trowel in her hand, working by a gravestone. Hoke, jacket in hand, sleeves rolled up, stands nearby.

HOKE: I jes' thinkin', Miz Daisy. We bin out heah to the cemetery three times dis mont' already and ain' even the twentieth yet.

DAISY: It's good to come in nice weather.

HOKE: Yassum. Mist' Sig's grave mighty well tended. I b'lieve you the best widow in the state of Georgia.

DAISY: Boolie's always pestering me to let the staff out here tend to this plot. Perpetual care they call it.

HOKE: Doan' you do it. It right to have somebody from the family lookin' after you.

DAISY: I'll certainly never have that. Boolie will have me in perpetual care before I'm cold.

HOKE: Come on now, Miz Daisy.

DAISY: Hoke, run back to the car and get that pot of azaleas for me and set it on Leo Bauer's grave.

HOKE: Miz Rose Bauer's husband?

DAISY: That's right. She asked me to bring it out here for her. She's not very good about coming. And I believe today would've been Leo's birthday.

HOKE: Yassum. Where the grave at?

DAISY: I'm not exactly sure. But I know it's over that way on the other side of the weeping cherry. You'll see the headstone. Bauer.

HOKE: Yassum.

DAISY: What's the matter?

HOKE: Nothin' the matter.

He exits. She works with her trowel. In a moment Hoke returns with flowers.

Miz Daisy . . .

DAISY: I told you it's over on the other side of the weeping cherry. It says Bauer on the headstone.

HOKE: How'd that look?

DAISY: What are you talking about?

HOKE *(Deeply embarrassed)*: I'm talkin' 'bout I cain' read.

DAISY: What?

HOKE: I cain' read.

DAISY: That's ridiculous. Anybody can read.

HOKE: Nome. Not me.

DAISY: Then how come I see you looking at the paper all the time?

HOKE: That's it. Jes' lookin'. I dope out what's happening from the pictures.

DAISY: You know your letters, don't you?

HOKE: My ABCs. Yassum, pretty good. I jes' cain' read.

DAISY: Stop saying that. It's making me mad. If you know your letters then you can read. You just don't know you can read. I taught some of the stupidest children God ever put on the face of this earth and all of them could read enough to find a name on a tombstone. The name is Bauer. Buh buh buh buh Bauer. What does that buh letter sound like?

HOKE: Sound like a B.

DAISY: Of course. Buh Bauer. Er er er er er. Bau-*er*. That's the last part. What letter sounds like er?

HOKE: R?

DAISY: So the first letter is a—

HOKE: B.

DAISY: And the last letter is an—

HOKE: R.

DAISY: B-R. B-R. B-R. Brr. Brr. Brr. It even sounds like Bauer, doesn't it?

HOKE: Sho' do Miz Daisy. Thass it?

DAISY: That's it. Now go over there like I told you in the first place and look for a headstone with a B at the beginning and an R at the end and that will be Bauer.

HOKE: We ain' gon worry 'bout what come in the middle?

DAISY: Not right now. This will be enough for you to find it. Go on now.

HOKE: Yassum.

DAISY: And don't come back here telling me you can't do it. You can.

HOKE: Miz Daisy . . .

DAISY: What now?

HOKE: I 'preciate this, Miz Daisy.

DAISY: Don't be ridiculous! I didn't do anything. Now, would you please hurry up? I'm burning up out here.

Light goes out on them and in the dark we hear Eartha Kitt singing "Santa Baby." Light up on Boolie. He wears a tweed jacket, red vest, holly in his lapel. He is on the phone.

BOOLIE: Mama? Merry Christmas. Listen, do Florine a favor, all right? She's having a fit and the grocery store is closed today. You got a package of coconut in your pantry? Would you bring it when you come? *(He calls offstage)* Hey, honey! Your ambrosia's saved! Mama's got the coconut! *(Back into the phone)* Many thanks. See you anon, Mama. Ho ho ho.

Lights out on Boolie and up on Daisy and Hoke in the car. Daisy is not in a festive mood.

HOKE: Ooooooh at them lit-up decorations!

DAISY: Everybody's giving the Georgia Power Company a Merry Christmas.

HOKE: Miz Florine's got 'em all beat with the lights.

DAISY: She makes an ass out of herself every year.

HOKE *(Loving it)*: Yassum.

DAISY: She always has to go and stick a wreath in every window she's got.

HOKE: Mmm-hmmm.

DAISY: And that silly Santa Claus winking on the front door!

HOKE: I bet she have the biggest tree in Atlanta. Where she get 'em so large?

DAISY: Absurd. If I had a nose like Florine I wouldn't go around saying Merry Christmas to anybody.

HOKE: I enjoy Christmas at they house.

DAISY: I don't wonder. You're the only Christian in the place!

HOKE: 'Cept they got that new cook.

DAISY: Florine never could keep help. Of course it's none of my affair.

HOKE: Nome.

DAISY: Too much running around. The Garden Club this and the Junior League that! As if any one of them would ever give her the time of day! But she'd die before she'd fix a glass of ice tea for the Temple Sisterhood!

HOKE: Yassum. You right.

DAISY: I just hope she doesn't take it in her head to sing this year. *(She imitates)* Glo-o-o-o-o-o-o-o-o-o-o-o-o-o-oriaaaa! She sounds like she has a bone stuck in her throat.

HOKE: You done say a mouthful, Miz Daisy.

DAISY: You didn't have to come. Boolie would've run me out.

HOKE: I know that.

DAISY: Then why did you?

HOKE: That my business, Miz Daisy. *(He turns into a driveway and stops the car)* Well, looka there! Miz Florine done put a Rudolph Reindeer in the dogwood tree.

DAISY: Oh my Lord! If her grandfather, old man Freitag,

could see this! What is it you say? I bet he'd jump
up out of his grave and snatch her baldheaded!

Hoke opens the door for Daisy.

Wait a minute. *(She takes a small package wrapped in
brown paper from her purse)* This isn't a Christmas
present.

HOKE: Nome.

DAISY: You know I don't give Christmas presents.

HOKE: I sho' do.

DAISY: I just happened to run across it this morning.
Open it up.

HOKE *(Unwrapping package)*: Ain' nobody ever give me a
book. *(Laboriously reads the cover)* Handwriting Copy
Book—Grade Five.

DAISY: I always taught out of these. I saved a few.

HOKE: Yassum.

DAISY: It's faded but it works. If you practice, you'll
write nicely.

HOKE *(Trying not to show emotion)*: Yassum.

DAISY: But you have to practice. I taught Mayor
Hartsfield out of this same book.

HOKE: Thank you, Miz Daisy.

DAISY: It's not a Christmas present.

HOKE: Nome.

DAISY: Jews don't have any business giving Christmas
presents. And you don't need to go yapping about
this to Boolie and Florine.

HOKE: This strictly between you and me.

We hear a record of "Rudolph the Red-Nosed Reindeer."

They seen us. Mist' Werthan done turn up the hi-fi.

DAISY: I hope I don't spit up.

Hoke takes her arm and they walk off together as the light fades on them. Light up on Boolie, wearing madras bermuda shorts and Lacoste shirt. He is in his late forties, waiting by the car.

BOOLIE *(Calling)*: Come on, Hoke! Get a wiggle on! I'm supposed to tee off at the club at 11:30.

Hoke enters.

HOKE: Jes' emptyin' the trash. Sad'dy garbage day, you know.

BOOLIE: Where's Mama?

HOKE: She back in her room and she say go on widdout her. I think she takin' on 'bout dis.

They have gotten in the car, both in the front seat. Hoke is driving.

BOOLIE: That's crazy. A car is a car.

HOKE: Yassuh, but she done watch over dis machine like a chicken hawk. One day we park in front of de dry cleaner up yonder at the Plaza and dis white man— look like some kind of lawyer, banker, dress up real fine—he done lay his satchel up on our hood while he open up his trunk, you know, and Lawd what he do that for, fore I could stop her, yo' mama jump out de back do' and run that man every which way. She wicked 'bout her paint job.

BOOLIE: Did she tell you this new car has air conditioning?

HOKE: She say she doan' like no air-cool. Say it give her the neckache.

BOOLIE: Well, you know how Mama fought me, but it's time for a trade. She's losing equity on this car. I bet both of you will miss this old thing.

HOKE: Not me. Unh-unh.

BOOLIE: Oh come on. You're the only one that's driven it all this time. Aren't you just a little sorry to see it go?

HOKE: It ain' goin' nowhere. I done bought it.

BOOLIE: You didn't!

HOKE: I already made the deal with Mist' Red Mitchell at the car place.

BOOLIE: For how much?

HOKE: Dat for him and me to know.

BOOLIE: For God's sake! Why didn't you just buy it right from Mama? You'd have saved money.

HOKE: Yo' mama in my business enough as it is. I ain' studyin' makin' no monthly car payments to her. Dis mine the regular way.

BOOLIE: It's a good car, all right. I guess nobody knows that better than you.

HOKE: Best ever come off the line. And dis new one, Miz Daisy doan' take to it, I let her ride in disheah now an' again.

BOOLIE: Mighty nice of you.

HOKE: Well, we all doin' what we can. Keep them ashes off my 'polstry.

Light out on them and up on Daisy's driveway. Daisy, wearing traveling clothes and a hat, enters lugging a big heavy suitcase. She looks around anxiously, checks her watch and exits again. In a moment she returns with a full dress bag and a picnic basket. She sets them by the suitcase, looks around, becoming more agitated, and exits again. Now she returns with a large elaborately wrapped package. Hoke enters, carrying a small suitcase.

DAISY: It's three after seven.

HOKE: Yassum. You say we leavin' at fifteen to eight.

DAISY: At the latest, I said.

HOKE: Now what bizness you got draggin' disheah out de house by yo'seff?

DAISY: Who was here to help me?

HOKE: Miz Daisy, it doan' take mo'n five minutes to load up de trunk. You fixin' to break both yo' arms and yo' legs too fo' we even get outta Atlanta. You takin' on too much.

DAISY: I hate doing things at the last minute.

HOKE: What you talkin' 'bout? You ready to go fo' the las' week and half! *(He picks up the present)*

DAISY: Don't touch that.

HOKE: Ain' it wrap pretty. Dat Mist' Walter's present?

DAISY: Yes. It's fragile. I'll hold it on the seat with me.

Boolie enters carrying his briefcase and a small wrapped package.

Well, you nearly missed us!

BOOLIE: I thought you were leaving at quarter of.

HOKE: She takin' on.

DAISY: Be still.

BOOLIE: Florine sent this for Uncle Walter. *(Daisy recoils from it)* Well, it's not a snake, Mama. I think it's notepaper.

DAISY: How appropriate. Uncle Walter can't see!

BOOLIE: Maybe it's soap.

DAISY: How nice that you show such an interest in your uncle's ninetieth birthday.

BOOLIE: Don't start up, Mama. I cannot go to Mobile with you. I have to go to New York tonight for the convention. You know that.

DAISY: The convention starts Monday. And I know what else I know.

BOOLIE: Just leave Florine out of it. She wrote away for those tickets eight months ago.

DAISY: I'm sure *My Fair Lady* is more important than your own flesh and blood.

BOOLIE: Mama!

DAISY: Those Christians will be mighty impressed!

BOOLIE: I can't talk to you when you're like this.

Daisy has climbed into the car. Boolie draws Hoke aside.

I've got to talk to Hoke.

DAISY: They expect us for a late supper in Mobile.

BOOLIE: You'll be there.

DAISY: I know they'll fix crab. All that trouble!

BOOLIE *(To Hoke)*: I don't know how you're going to stand all day in the car.

HOKE: She doan' mean nothin'. She jes' worked up.

BOOLIE: Here's fifty dollars in case you run into trouble. Don't show it to Mama. You've got your map?

HOKE: She got it in wid her. Study every inch of the way.

BOOLIE: I'll be at the Ambassador Hotel in New York. On Park Avenue.

DAISY: It's seven sixteen.

BOOLIE: You should have a job on the radio announcing the time.

DAISY: I want to miss rush hour.

BOOLIE: Congratulate Uncle Walter for me. And kiss everybody in Mobile.

DAISY (*To Hoke*): Did you have the air condition checked? I told you to have the air condition checked!

HOKE: Yassum. I got the air condition checked but I doan' know what for. You doan' never 'low me to turn it on.

DAISY: Hush up.

BOOLIE: Good-bye! Good luck! (*Light out on the car*) Good God!

Light out on Boolie and back up on the car. It's lunchtime. Daisy and Hoke are both eating. Hoke eats while he drives.

HOKE: Idella stuff eggs good.

DAISY: You stuff yourself good. I'm going to save the rest of this for later.

HOKE: Yassum.

DAISY: I was thinking about the first time I ever went to Mobile. It was Walter's wedding, 1888.

HOKE: 1888! You weren't nothin' but a little child.

DAISY: I was twelve. We went on the train. And I was so excited. I'd never been on a train, I'd never been in a wedding party and I'd never seen the ocean. Papa said it was the Gulf of Mexico and not the ocean,

but it was all the same to me. I remember we were
at a picnic somewhere — somebody must have taken
us all bathing — and I asked Papa if it was all right
to dip my hand in the water. He laughed because I
was so timid. And then I tasted the salt water on my
fingers. Isn't it silly to remember that?

HOKE: No sillier than most of what folks remember. You
talkin' 'bout first time. I tell you 'bout the first time
I ever leave the state of Georgia?

DAISY: When was that?

HOKE: 'Bout twenty-five minutes back.

DAISY: Go on!

HOKE: Thass right. First time. My daughter, she married
to Pullman porter on the N.C. & St. L., you know,
and she all time goin' — Detroit, New York, St.
Louis — talkin' 'bout snow up aroun' her waist and
ridin' in de subway car and I say, "Well, that very
nice Tommie Lee, but I jes' doan' feel the need." So
dis it, Miz Daisy, and I got to tell you, Alabama ain'
lookin' like much so far.

DAISY: It's nicer the other side of Montgomery.

HOKE: If you say so. Pass me up one of them peaches,
please ma'am.

She looks out the window. Suddenly she starts.

DAISY: Oh my God!

HOKE: What happen?

DAISY: That sign said Phenix City — thirty miles. We're
not supposed to go to Phenix City. We're going the
wrong way. Oh my God!

HOKE: Maybe you done read it wrong.

DAISY: I didn't. Stop the car! Stop the car! *(Very agitated, she wrestles with the map on her lap)* Here! Here! You took the wrong turn at Opelika!

HOKE: You took it with me. And you readin' the map.

DAISY: I was getting the lunch. Go on back! Oh my God!

HOKE: It ain't been thirty minutes since we turn.

DAISY: I'm such a fool! I didn't have any business coming in the car by myself with just you. Boolie made me! I should have come on the train. I'd be safe there. I just should have come on the train.

HOKE: Yassum. You should have.

Lights dim to suggest passage of time and come right back up again. It is night now. Daisy and Hoke are somewhat slumped on the seats, Hoke driving wearily.

DAISY: They fixed crab for me. Minnie always fixes crab. They go to so much trouble! It's all ruined by now! Oh Lord!

HOKE: We got to pull over, Miz Daisy.

DAISY: Is something wrong with the car?

HOKE: Nome. I got to bixcused.

DAISY: What?

HOKE: I got to make water.

DAISY: You should have thought of that back at the Standard Oil Station.

HOKE: Colored cain' use the toilet at no Standard Oil. . . . You know dat.

DAISY: Well there's no time to stop. We'll be in Mobile soon. You can wait.

HOKE: Yassum. *(He drives a minute then stops the car)* Nome.

DAISY: I told you to wait!

HOKE: Yassum. I hear you. How you think I feel havin' to ax you when can I make my water like I some damn dog?

DAISY: Why, Hoke! I'd be ashamed!

HOKE: I ain't no dog and I ain' no chile and I ain' jes' a back of the neck you look at while you goin' wherever you want to go. I a man nearly seventy-two years old and I know when my bladder full and I gettin' out dis car and goin' off down de road like I got to do. And I'm takin' de car key dis time. And that's de end of it.

He leaves the car, slamming his door, and exits. Daisy sits very still in the back seat. It's a dark country night. Crickets chirp, a dog barks.

DAISY *(Angry)*: Hoke! *(She waits. No sound. Then, less angry)* Hoke! *(Silence. Darkness. Country sounds. Now she is frightened)* Hoke?

No answer. Light fades on her slowly and comes up on Boolie, in his office. He speaks into his phone in answer to an intercom buzz.

BOOLIE: Well, hell yes! Send him right on in here!

Hoke enters.

Isn't it your day off? To what do I owe this honor?

HOKE: We got to talk.

BOOLIE: What is it?

HOKE: It Mist' Sinclair Harris.

BOOLIE: My cousin Sinclair?

HOKE: His wife.

BOOLIE: Jeanette?

HOKE: The one talk funny.

BOOLIE: She's from Canton, Ohio.

HOKE: Yassuh. She tryin' to hire me.

BOOLIE: What?

HOKE: She phone when she know Miz Daisy be out and she say "How are they treating you, Hoke?" You know how she soun' like her nose stuff up. And I say "Fine" and she say "Well, if you looking for a change you know where to call."

BOOLIE: I'll be damned!

HOKE: I thought you want to know 'bout it.

BOOLIE: I'll be goddamned!

HOKE: Ain't she a mess? *(A beat)* She say name yo' sal'ry.

BOOLIE: I see. And did you?

HOKE: Did I what?

BOOLIE: Name your salary?

HOKE: Now what you think I am? I ain' studyin' workin' for no trashy somethin' like her.

BOOLIE: But she got you to thinking, didn't she?

HOKE: You might could say dat.

BOOLIE: Name your salary?

HOKE: Dat what she say.

BOOLIE: Well, how does sixty-five dollars a week sound?

HOKE: Sounds pretty good. Seventy-five sounds better.

BOOLIE: So it does. Beginning this week.

HOKE: Das mighty nice of you Mist' Werthan. I 'preciate it. Mist' Werthan, you ever had people fightin' over you?

BOOLIE: No.

HOKE: Well, I tell you. It feel good.

Light out on them. We hear a phone ringing. Light up on Daisy's house. It's a dark, winter morning and there is no light on in the house. Daisy enters, wearing her coat over her bathrobe and carrying a lit candle in a candlestick. She is up in her eighties now and walks more carefully, but she is by no means decrepit.

DAISY: Hello?

Light up on Boolie at home, also dressed warmly.

BOOLIE: Mama, thank goodness! I was afraid your phone would be out.
DAISY: No, but I don't have any power.
BOOLIE: Nobody does. That's why I called.
DAISY: I found some candles. It reminds me of gaslight back on Forsyth Street. Seems like we had ice storms all the time back then.
BOOLIE: I can't come after you because my driveway is a sheet of ice. I'm sure yours is too.
DAISY: I'm all right, Boolie.
BOOLIE: I imagine they're working on the lines now. I'll go listen to my car radio and call you back. Don't go anywhere.
DAISY: Really? I thought I'd take a jog around the neighborhood.
BOOLIE: You're a doodle, Mama.
DAISY: Love to Florine.
BOOLIE: Uh-huh.

Light out on Boolie. Daisy talks to herself.

34

DAISY: Well, I guess that's the biggest lie I'll tell today.

She tries to read by the candlelight without much success. She hears the door to outside open and close and then footsteps. She stands alarmed.

Who is it?

Hoke enters carrying a paper bag and wearing an overcoat and galoshes.

HOKE: Mornin' Miz Daisy.

DAISY: Hoke. What in the world?

HOKE: I learn to drive on ice when I deliver milk for Avondale Dairy. Ain' much to it. I slip around a little comin' down Briarcliff, but nothin' happen. Other folks bangin' into each other like they in the funny papers, though. Oh, I stop at the 7–11. I figure yo' stove out and Lawd knows you got to have yo' coffee in the mornin'.

DAISY *(Touched)*: How sweet of you, Hoke.

He sips his own coffee.

HOKE: We ain' had good coffee roun' heah since Idella pass.

DAISY: You're right. I can fix her biscuits and you can fry her chicken, but nobody can make Idella's coffee. I wonder how she did it.

HOKE: I doan' nome. Every time the Hit Parade come on TV, it put me in mind of Idella.

DAISY: Yes.

HOKE: Sittin' up in de chair, her daughter say, spry as de flowers in springtime, watchin' the Hit Parade like

she done ev'ry Sad'dy the Lawd sent and then, durin'
the Lucky Strike Extra all of sudden, she belch and
she gone.

DAISY: Idella was lucky.

HOKE: Yassum. I 'spec she was. *(He starts to exit)*

DAISY: Where are you going?

HOKE: Put deseheah things up. Take off my overshoes.

DAISY: I didn't think you'd come today.

HOKE: What you mean? It ain' my day off, is it?

DAISY: Well, I don't know what you can do around here
except keep me company.

HOKE: I see can I light us a fire.

DAISY: Eat anything you want out of the icebox. It's all
going to spoil anyway.

HOKE: Yassum.

DAISY: And wipe up what you tracked onto my kitchen
floor.

HOKE: Now Miz Daisy, what you think I am? A mess?
*(This is an old routine between them and not without
affection)*

DAISY: Yes. That's exactly what I think you are.

HOKE: All right, then. All right.

He exits. She sits contented in her chair. The phone rings.

DAISY: Hello?

Light on Boolie.

BOOLIE: It'll all be melted by this afternoon. They said
so on the radio. I'll be out after you as soon as I can
get down the driveway.

DAISY: Stay where you are, Boolie. Hoke is here with me.

BOOLIE: How in the hell did he manage that?

DAISY: He's very handy. I'm fine. I don't need a thing in the world.

BOOLIE: Hello? Have I got the right number? I never heard you say loving things about Hoke before.

DAISY: I didn't say I love him. I said he was handy.

BOOLIE: Uh-huh.

DAISY: Honestly, Boolie. Are you trying to irritate me in the middle of an ice storm?

She hangs up the phone. Light out on her. Boolie stands a moment in wonder. Light out on him. In the dark we hear the sounds of horns blaring. A serious traffic jam. When the lights come up, Daisy is in the car, wearing a hat. She is anxious, twisting in her seat, looking out the window. Hoke enters.

Well what is it? You took so long!

HOKE: Couldn't help it. Big mess up yonder.

DAISY: What's the matter? I might as well not go to temple at all now!

HOKE: You cain' go to temple today, Miz Daisy.

DAISY: Why not? What in the world is the matter with you?

HOKE: Somebody done bomb the temple.

DAISY: What? Bomb the temple!

HOKE: Yassum. Dat why we stuck here so long.

DAISY: I don't believe it.

HOKE: That what the policeman tell me up yonder. Say it happen about a half hour ago.

DAISY: Oh no. Oh my God! Well, was anybody there? Were people hurt?

HOKE: Din' say.

DAISY: Who would do that?

HOKE: You know as good as me. Always be the same ones.

DAISY: Well, it's a mistake. I'm sure they meant to bomb one of the conservative synagogues or the orthodox one. The temple is reform. Everybody knows that.

HOKE: It doan' matter to them people. A Jew is a Jew to them folks. Jes' like light or dark we all the same nigger.

DAISY: I can't believe it!

HOKE: I know jes' how you feel, Miz Daisy. Back down there above Macon on the farm—I 'bout ten or 'leven years old and one day my frien' Porter, his daddy hangin' from a tree. And the day befo', he laughin' and pitchin' horseshoes wid us. Talkin' 'bout Porter and me gon have strong good right arms like him and den he hangin' up yonder wid his hands tie behind his back an' the flies all over him. And I seed it with my own eyes and I throw up right where I standin'. You go on and cry.

DAISY: I'm not crying.

HOKE: Yassum.

DAISY: The idea! Why did you tell me that?

HOKE: I doan' know. Seem like disheah mess put me in mind of it.

DAISY: Ridiculous! The temple has nothing to do with that!

HOKE: So you say.

DAISY: We don't even know what happened. How do you know that policeman was telling the truth?

HOKE: Now why would that policeman go and lie 'bout a thing like that?

DAISY: You never get things right anyway.

HOKE: Miz Daisy, somebody done bomb that place and you know it too.

DAISY: Go on. Just go on now. I don't want to hear any more about it.

HOKE: I see if I can get us outta here and take you home. You feel better at home.

DAISY: I don't feel bad.

HOKE: You de boss.

DAISY: Stop talking to me!

Lights fade on them. We hear the sound of applause. Boolie enters in a fine three-piece suit, holding a large silver bowl. He is very distinguished, in his late fifties.

BOOLIE: Thank you, Red. And thank you all. I am deeply grateful to be chosen man of the year by the Atlanta Business Council, an honor I've seen bestowed on some mighty fine fellas and which I certainly never expected to come to me. I'm afraid the loss here, *(He touches his hair)* and the gain here, *(He touches his belly)* have given me an air of competence I don't possess. But I'll tell you, I sure wish my father and my grandfather could see this. Seventy-two years ago they opened a little hole-in-the-wall shop on Whitehall Street with one printing press. They managed to grow with Atlanta and to this day, the Werthan Company believes we want what Atlanta wants. This award proves we must be right. Thank you. *(Applause)* One more thing. If the

Jackets whup the Dawgs up in Athens Saturday
afternoon, I'll be a completely happy man.

*Light out on him. Daisy enters her living room and dials
the phone. She dials with some difficulty. Things have
become harder for her to do.*

DAISY: Hidey, Miss McClatchey. You always recognize
my voice. What a shame a wonderful girl like you
never married. Miss McClatchey? Is my son in? Oh
no. Please don't call him out of a sales meeting. Just
give him a message. Tell him I bought the tickets
for the UJA banquet. Yes, UJA banquet honoring
Martin Luther King on the seventeenth. Well, you're
a sweet thing to say so. And don't you worry. My
cousin Tillie in Chattanooga married for the first
time at fifty-seven.

Light dims and comes right back. Boolie has joined Daisy.

BOOLIE: How do you feel, Mama?
DAISY: Not a good question to ask somebody nearly
ninety.
BOOLIE: Well you look fine.
DAISY: It's my ageless appeal.
BOOLIE: Miss McClatchey gave me your message.
DAISY: Florine is invited too.
BOOLIE: Thank you very much.
DAISY: I guess Hoke should drive us. There'll be a crowd.
BOOLIE: Mama, we have to talk about this.
DAISY: Talk about what?
BOOLIE: The feasibility of all this.
DAISY: Fine. You drive. I thought I was being helpful.

BOOLIE: You know I believe Martin Luther King has
done some mighty fine things.

DAISY: Boolie, if you don't want to go, why don't you
just come right out and say so?

BOOLIE: I want to go. You know how I feel about him.

DAISY: Of course, but Florine—

BOOLIE: Florine has nothing to do with it. I still have to
conduct business in this town.

DAISY: I see. The Werthan Company will go out of
business if you attend the King dinner?

BOOLIE: Not exactly. But a lot of the men I do business
with wouldn't like it. They wouldn't come right out
and say so. They'd just snicker and call me Martin
Luther Werthan behind my back—something like
that. And I'd begin to notice that my banking
business wasn't being handled by the top dogs.
Maybe I'd start to miss out on a few special favors, a
few tips. I wouldn't hear about certain lunch
meetings at the Commerce Club. Little things you
can't quite put your finger on. And Jack Raphael
over at Ideal Press, he's a New York Jew instead of a
Georgia Jew and as long as you got to deal with
Jews, the really smart ones come from New York,
don't they? So some of the boys might start throwing
business to Jack instead of ole Martin Luther
Werthan. I don't know. Maybe it wouldn't happen,
but that's the way it works. If we don't use those
seats, somebody else will and the good Doctor King
will never know the difference, will he?

DAISY: If we don't use the seats? I'm not supposed to go
either?

BOOLIE: Mama, you can do whatever you want.

DAISY: Thanks for your permission.

BOOLIE: Can I ask you something? When did you get so fired up about Martin Luther King? Time was, I'd have heard a different story.

DAISY: Why, Boolie! I've never been prejudiced and you know it!

BOOLIE: Okay. Why don't you ask Hoke to go to the dinner with you?

DAISY: Hoke? Don't be ridiculous. He wouldn't go.

BOOLIE: Ask him and see.

Boolie exits. Daisy puts on an evening wrap and a chiffon scarf over her hair. This is not done quickly. She moves slowly. When she is ready, Hoke enters and helps her into the car. They ride in silence for a moment.

DAISY: I don't know why you still drive. You can't see.

HOKE: Yassum I can.

DAISY: You didn't see that mailbox.

HOKE: How you know what I didn't see?

DAISY: It nearly poked through my window. This car is all scratched up.

HOKE: Ain' no sucha thing.

DAISY: How would you know? You can't see. What a shame. It's a bran' new car, too.

HOKE: You got this car two years come March.

DAISY: You forgot to turn.

HOKE: Ain' this dinner at the Biltmo'?

DAISY: You know it is.

HOKE: Biltmo' straight thissaway.

DAISY: You know so much.

HOKE: Yassum. I do.

DAISY: I've lived in Atlanta all my life.

HOKE: And ain' run a car in onto twenty years.

A beat.

DAISY: Boolie said the silliest thing the other day.

HOKE: Tha' right?

DAISY: He's too old to be so foolish.

HOKE: Yassum. What did he say?

DAISY: Oh, he was talking about Martin Luther King. *(A beat)* I guess you know him, don't you?

HOKE: Martin Luther King? Nome.

DAISY: I was sure you did. But you've heard him preach?

HOKE: Same way as you—over the TV.

DAISY: I think he's wonderful.

HOKE: Yassum.

DAISY: You know, you could go see him in person anytime you wanted. *(No response)* All you'd have to do is go over there to the—what is it?

HOKE: Ebeneezer.

DAISY: Ebeneezer Baptist Church some Sunday and there he'll be.

HOKE: What you gettin' at, Miz Daisy?

DAISY: Well, it's so silly. Boolie said you wanted to go to this dinner with me tonight. Did you tell him that?

HOKE: Nome.

DAISY: I didn't think so. What would be the point? You can hear him anytime—whenever you want.

HOKE: You want the front do' or the side do' to the Biltmore?

43

DAISY: I think the side. Isn't it wonderful the way things are changing?

HOKE: What you think I am, Miz Daisy?

DAISY: What do you mean?

HOKE: You think I some somethin' sittin' up here doan' know nothin' 'bout how to do?

DAISY: I don't know what you're talking about.

HOKE: Invitation to disheah dinner come in the mail a mont' ago. Did be you want me to go wid you, how come you wait till we in the car on the way to ask me?

DAISY: What? All I said was that Boolie said you wanted to go.

HOKE (Sulking): Mmm-hmmm.

DAISY: You know you're welcome to come, Hoke.

HOKE: Mmmm-hmmm.

DAISY: Oh my stars. Well, aren't you a great big baby!

HOKE: Nevermind baby, next time you ask me someplace, ask me regular.

DAISY: You don't have to carry on so much!

HOKE: Das all. Less drop it.

DAISY: Honestly!

HOKE: Things changin', but they ain't change all dat much. (They are at the door) I hep you to the do'.

DAISY: Thank you, Hoke. I can help myself.

Daisy gets herself out of the car, which takes some effort. Hoke sits still in his seat. Daisy looks at him when she is out of the car, but thinks better of what she was going to say and walks slowly towards the door. Lights out on them and up on Boolie at his house.

44

BOOLIE *(On the phone)*: Hello, Hoke? How are you?

HOKE: I'm tolerable, Mist' Werthan.

BOOLIE: What can I do for you this morning?

HOKE: It yo' mama.

BOOLIE: What's the matter?

HOKE: She worked up.

BOOLIE: Why should today be different from any other day?

HOKE: No, this ain' the same.

DAISY *(Offstage)*: Hoke?

HOKE: Yassum? *(Back to phone)* She think she teachin' school. I'm real worried 'bout her. She ain' makin' sense.

BOOLIE: I'll be right there.

Lights out on Boolie. He exits. Daisy enters. She is in disarray. Her hair is not combed and her housecoat is open, the slip showing underneath.

DAISY: Hoke? Hoke?

HOKE: Yassum?

DAISY: Where did you put my papers?

HOKE: Ain' no papers, Miz Daisy.

DAISY: My papers! I had them all corrected last night and I put them in the front so I wouldn't forget them on my way to school. What did you do with them?

HOKE: You talkin' outta yo' head.

DAISY: The children will be so disappointed if I don't give them their homework back. I always give it back the next day. That's why they like me. Why aren't you helping me?

HOKE: What you want me to do, Miz Daisy?

DAISY: Give me the papers. I told you. It's all right if
you moved them. I won't be mad with you. But I've
got to get to school now. I'll be late and who will
take care of my class? They'll be all alone. Oh God!
Oh Goddy! I do everything wrong.

HOKE: Set down. You about to fall and hurt yo'seff.

DAISY: It doesn't matter. I'm sorry. It's all my fault. I
didn't do right. It's so awful! Oh God!

HOKE: Now you lissen heah. Ain' nothin' awful 'cep the
way you carryin' on.

DAISY: I'm so sorry. It's all my fault. I can't find the
papers and the children are waiting.

HOKE: No they ain'. You ain' no teacher no mo'.

DAISY: It doesn't make any difference.

HOKE: Miz Daisy, ain' nothin' the matter wit' you.

DAISY: You don't know. You don't know. What's the
difference?

HOKE: Your mind done took a turn this mornin' thass
all.

DAISY: Go on. Just go on now.

HOKE: You snap right back if you jes' let yo'seff.

DAISY: I can't! I can't!

HOKE: You a lucky ole woman, you know dat?

DAISY: No! No! It's all a mess now. And I can't do
anything about it!

HOKE: You rich, you well for your time and you got
people care about what happen to you.

DAISY: I'm being trouble. Oh God, I don't want to be
trouble to anybody.

HOKE: You want something to cry about, I take you to

the state home, show you what layin' out dere in de halls.

DAISY: Oh my God!

HOKE: An' I bet none of them take on bad as you doin'.

DAISY: I'm sorry. I'm so sorry. Those poor children in my class.

HOKE: You keep dis up, I promise, Mist' Werthan call the doctor on you and just as sho' as you born, that doctor gon have you in de insane asylum fore you know what hit you. Dat de way you want it to be?

Daisy looks at him. She speaks in her normal voice.

DAISY: Hoke, do you still have that Oldsmobile?

HOKE: From when I firs' come here? Go on, Miz Daisy, that thing been in the junkyard fifteen years or more. I drivin' yo' next-to-las' car now, '63 Cadillac, runnin' fine as wine.

DAISY: You ought not to be driving anything, the way you see.

HOKE: How you know the way I see, 'less you lookin' outta my eyes?

DAISY: Hoke?

HOKE: Yassum?

DAISY: You're my best friend.

HOKE: Come on, Miz Daisy. You jes' —

DAISY: No. Really. You are. You are. *(She takes his hand)*

HOKE: Yassum.

The light fades on them. Boolie enters. He is sixty-five now. He walks slowly around Daisy's living room, picking up a book here and there, examining an ashtray. He leafs

through his mother's little leather phone book and puts it in
his pocket. Hoke enters. He is eighty-five. He shuffles a bit
and his glasses are very thick.

HOKE: Mornin' Mist' Werthan.

BOOLIE: Well Hoke, good to see you. You didn't drive
yourself out here?

HOKE: Nawsuh. I doan' drive now. My granddaughter
run me out.

BOOLIE: My Lord, is she old enough to drive?

HOKE: Michelle thirty-seven. Teach biology at Spelman
College.

BOOLIE: I never knew that.

HOKE: Yassuh.

BOOLIE: I've taken most of what I want out of the house.
Is there anything you'd like before the Goodwill
comes?

HOKE: My place full to burstin' now.

BOOLIE: It feels funny to sell the house while Mama's still
alive.

HOKE: I 'gree.

BOOLIE: But she hasn't even been inside the door for two
years. I know I'm doing the right thing.

HOKE: Doan' get me into it.

BOOLIE: I'm not going to say anything to her about it.

HOKE: You right there.

BOOLIE: By the way, Hoke, your check is going to keep
coming every week—as long as you're there to get it.

HOKE: I 'preciate that, Mist' Werthan.

BOOLIE: You can rest easy about it. I suppose you don't
get out to see Mama very much.

HOKE: It hard, not drivin'. Dat place ain' on no bus line. I goes in a taxicab sometime.

BOOLIE: I'm sure she appreciates it.

HOKE: Some days she better than others. Who ain't?

BOOLIE: Well, we'd better get on out there. I guess you have a turkey dinner to get to and so do I. Why don't we call your granddaughter and tell her I'll run you home?

They exit and the light comes up on Daisy, ninety-seven, slowly moving forward with a walker. She seems fragile and diminished, but still vital. A hospital chair and a table are nearby. Boolie and Hoke join her.

Happy Thanksgiving, Mama. Look who I brought.

Boolie helps Daisy from her walker into her chair.

HOKE: Mornin', Miz Daisy. *(She nods)* You keepin' yo'seff busy?

Silence.

BOOLIE: She certainly is. She goes to jewelry making — how many times a week is it, Mama? She makes all kinds of things. Pins and bracelets. She's a regular Tiffanys.

HOKE: Ain't that something.

Daisy seems far away.

BOOLIE *(Keeping things going)*: Hoke, you know I thought of you the other morning on the Expressway. I saw an Avondale milk truck.

HOKE: You doan' say.

BOOLIE: A big monster of a thing, must've had sixteen wheels. I wonder how you'd have liked driving that around.

DAISY *(Suddenly)*: Hoke came to see me, not you.

HOKE: This one of her good days.

BOOLIE: Florine says to wish you a Happy Thanksgiving. She's in Washington, you know. *(No response)* You remember, Mama. She's a Republican National Committeewoman now.

DAISY: Good God! *(Hoke laughs, Boolie grins)* Boolie!

BOOLIE: What is it, Mama?

DAISY: Go charm the nurses.

BOOLIE *(To Hoke)*: She wants you all to herself. *(To Daisy)* You're a doodle, Mama.

Boolie exits. Daisy dozes for a minute in her chair. Then she looks at Hoke.

DAISY: Boolie payin' you still?

HOKE: Every week.

DAISY: How much?

HOKE: That between me an' him, Miz Daisy.

DAISY: Highway robbery. *(She closes her eyes again. Then opens them)* How are you?

HOKE: Doin' the bes' I can.

DAISY: Me too.

HOKE: Well, thass all there is to it, then.

She nods, smiles. Silence. He sees the piece of pie on the table.

Looka here. You ain' eat yo' Thanksgiving pie.

She tries to pick up her fork. Hoke takes the plate and fork from her.

Lemme hep you wid this.

He cuts a small piece of pie with the fork and gently feeds it to her. Then another as the lights fade slowly out.

END OF PLAY